Learn & Play

Sudoku

for Fourth Grade

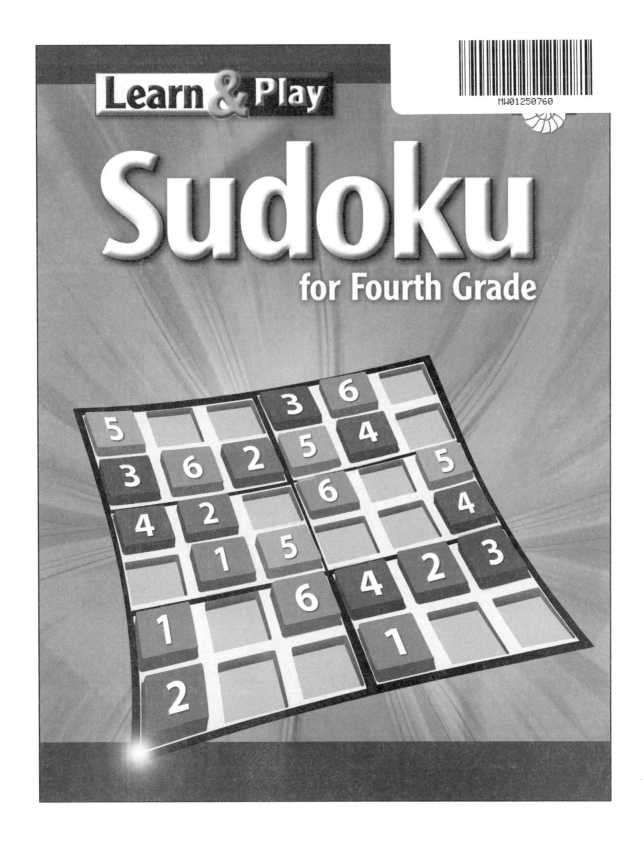

Author

Pamela Dase, M.A.Ed.

SHELL EDUCATION

Credits

Editorial Product Manager
Karie Feldner Gladis, M.S.Ed.

Assistant Editor
Torrey Maloof

Editorial Assistant
Kathryn R. Kiley

Editorial Director
Emily R. Smith, M.A.Ed.

Editor-in-Chief
Sharon Coan, M.S.Ed.

Editorial Manager
Gisela Lee, M.A.

Creative Director
Lee Aucoin

Cover Designer
Lesley Palmer

Illustration Manager
Timothy J. Bradley

Print Production
Phil Garcia
Don Tran

Interior Layout Designer
Robin Erickson

Publisher

Corinne Burton, M.A.Ed.

Shell Education
5301 Oceanus Drive
Huntington Beach, CA 92649-1030
http://www.shelleducation.com
ISBN 978-1-4258-0323-0

© 2007 Shell Education

Table of Contents

Introduction

What Is Sudoku? 4

The History of Sudoku 4

Sudoku Research 5

Learn to Play Sudoku 8

Strategies for Sudoku 9

How to Use This Book 11

Puzzle Variations at Each Grade Level . . 12

Correlations 12

Beginning Puzzles—Landforms

What a Jump! 14

Sheer Drop. 15

Sand Storm. 16

Freezing Cold. 17

Standing Tall. 18

Meandering Along 19

Prickly to the Touch 20

Keep Your Balance 21

Rolling On 22

Bird Watering Hole 23

Falling Down 24

Hard Edges. 25

Sandy Walk 26

Water Fountain 27

Close Quarters 28

Intermediate Puzzles—Decimals

Counting Your Pennies 30

Portion Control. 31

Exact Time 32

On Your Way 33

What a Bargain! 34

Feeling Sick? 35

Weighing In 36

What's the Total? 37

Play the Music 38

And the Total Is 39

Too Heavy? 40

Add It Up. 41

Run Fast 42

Tune It In 43

Ring It Up 44

Challenging Puzzles— American Indians

One-Room Home 46

Beautiful Baskets 47

Arrowheads 48

Music Maker 49

All Dressed Up. 50

Don't Look Down! 51

Colorful Clay 52

Rocky Pictures 53

Millions of Bison 54

Standing Straight 55

Northwestern Indians. 56

Animal Images 57

Powwow 58

Roaming Spirit 59

Painted Vessel. 60

Appendices

Appendix A: Templates. 61

Appendix B: Photograph Sources 64

Appendix C: Answer Key 65

What Is Sudoku?

Whether you are traveling or just relaxing on a Sunday morning, Sudoku is a pastime that the whole family can enjoy. The Sudoku craze has taken over. It is goodbye to crossword puzzles and magic squares. If you search the word *Sudoku* on Google™, you will get over 70 million hits. Sudoku puzzles are published in newspapers, magazines, and books. They even come in electronic handheld games or interactive games on the Web.

Source: TheSupe87/Shutterstock, Inc.

Sudoku is a logic puzzle. Each puzzle has one or more mini-grids. Each mini-grid has boxes that are arranged in rows and columns. Hints are given in some of the boxes. There are different types of puzzles. The puzzles can be 1 x 1 grids, 2 x 2 grids, 2 x 3 grids, 3 x 3 grids, or even more. Pictures, letters, and numbers are all used within the puzzles in this series.

The objective of a Sudoku puzzle is to fill in all the boxes of the puzzle using only the given hints. Each column, row, and mini-grid must have each picture, letter, or number only once. That means you have to pay attention to three things while you try to solve these puzzles. You have to look up and down the column, across the row, and around the mini-grid!

The History of Sudoku

How did the Sudoku craze start? Sudoku puzzles first appeared in a U.S. magazine in 1979. At that time it was called "number place." A magazine editor from Japan saw the number place puzzle and liked it so much that he decided to create a magazine with his version of it. He called the puzzle Sudoku. The word *su* in Japanese means *number,* and the word *doku* means *single*. The puzzle became very popular in Japan. Today, 660,000 Sudoku magazines are circulated every month in Japan.

Source: Daniel Gale/Shutterstock, Inc.

The Sudoku craze spread to the United Kingdom when Wayne Gould saw the puzzle in a magazine while working in Hong Kong. He was fascinated by the puzzles, so he created a computer program to generate Sudoku puzzles. Then, he sold his idea to the *London Times*. They used Gould's program to create a series for their daily games pages. Other newspapers then jumped on the bandwagon, spreading the craze back to the United States. In April 2005, Sudoku became a regular feature in the *New York Post*. *The Daily News* and *USA Today* followed a few months later.

The History of Sudoku *(cont.)*

Deep Roots

The puzzle goes back further than 1979. It actually has its roots in Latin Squares. Latin Squares were taken from the work of Swiss mathematician Leonhard Euler. He lived from 1707 to 1783. A Latin Square is a square grid that contains sets of different symbols repeated. The cells of the grid contain each symbol only once and the symbol can appear only once in each row and column. (Sound familiar?) Sudoku puzzles are really Latin Squares that have some of the symbols already filled in, and you have to fill in the rest. A set of Latin Squares is combined to form a Sudoku puzzle.

Portrait by Johann Georg Brucker

A Mental Sport

In 2006, the World Puzzle Federation held its first World Sudoku Championship. Like the Olympics, different countries send teams. There are both individual and team competitions. Each country can enter six participants plus one nonplaying captain. The participants have to solve different variations of Sudoku puzzles.

Find Out More

- What other number puzzles have similar rules to Sudoku?
- What other ideas have come from mathematician Leonhard Euler?

Sudoku Research

Sudoku is a kind of logic puzzle. No mathematical skills are needed to solve the puzzles, and you do not even need to use arithmetic. People solve the puzzles by logical reasoning alone (Sharp 2006). For this reason, these puzzles can be interesting and addictive for both children and adults alike. Not only are the puzzles a fun hobby, but the skills used to solve Sudoku puzzles can be transferred and applied to other areas of life.

For young people, the main benefit of solving Sudoku puzzles is the development of logical reasoning skills. These skills will help them solve math problems.

> There is a misconception that logical reasoning has nothing to do with mathematics. This seems to be tied to the idea that mathematics is about numbers. Indeed, Sudoku puzzles could have letters or colors or pictures instead of the numbers or any other property that comes with various attributes. (Sharp 2006)

Sudoku Research *(cont.)*

The heart of the puzzle, the mini-grid, is really a math problem about arrangements or combinations of objects (Sharp 2006). Logic is required in most areas of mathematics, and many examples of math problems can be given that require logical reasoning. Students can also use logical reasoning skills to find new ways to look at a problem and develop creative problem solving strategies.

To fully understand the depth of math concepts and become lifelong learners of mathematics, students need both logical reasoning and problem-solving skills. By solving Sudoku puzzles, students will begin to develop systematic thinking. They will learn to identify patterns and apply them. And, they will develop an awareness of the need to examine data carefully. These skills will also transfer over to other content areas, such as language acquisition. Puzzles are "well suited for contributing to a problem-based environment that is conducive to learning in the second-language classroom and may play an important role in the development of critical and higher-order thinking skills." Most importantly, puzzles offer second-language students the opportunity to repeat vocabulary and sentence structures in authentic contexts (Raizen 1999).

In the classroom, Sudoku puzzles are an easy way to differentiate instruction. The different grade levels of Sudoku can be used in one classroom. Each student can be given a puzzle from the grade level and skill level that bests suits his or her cognitive development of logical reasoning and problem-solving skills.

> Riddles and puzzles have broad appeal and are accessible to literally all ability levels. The conditions and objectives of the problems that are posed as puzzles are usually understood easily, although the solutions may be challenging. Even though some students may not be able to solve every puzzle, many enjoy the challenge of the attempt. (Evered 2001)

Students who have not been successful in mathematics can find success in solving Sudoku puzzles. In the preface to Raymond Smullyan's book, *The Lady or the Tiger and Other Logic Puzzles*, he states, "So many people I have met claim to hate math, and yet are enormously intrigued by any logic or math problem I give them, provided I present it in the form of a puzzle. I would not be at all surprised if good puzzle books prove to be one of the best cures for the so called, math anxiety" (1982).

Sudoku puzzles serve as an excellent warm-up activity, closing activity, problem-of-the day, enrichment activity, or break from the traditional curriculum content. Will Shortz, a puzzle creator and editor, states, "You can learn it in 10 seconds, and yet the logic needed to solve Sudoku is challenging. It's a perfect amount of time to spend on a puzzle, anywhere from five minutes to half an hour" (Bennett 2006).

Sudoku Research *(cont.)*

The puzzles are engaging and addictive for students. Filling in the empty cells appeals to them, and the rush at the very end to complete the puzzle gives them a great feeling of accomplishment. This inherent element of solving the puzzle adds a level of excitement to the classroom and is an intrinsic motivator for students (Evered 2001). The puzzle serves as a catalyst for learning (Raizen 1999).

Source: Ramon Berk/Shutterstock, Inc.

For both adults and students, Sudoku is a way to sharpen your brain and improve your focus. It requires concentration, patience, and self-discipline. According to Shortz, "You have to be focused to be a good Sudoku solver, because if you make a mistake and then base further logic on the mistake you made you have no option but to erase everything and start over. So Sudoku really teaches you to be careful" (Bennett 2006). Sudoku can also be a way to reduce stress or anxiety. While working on the puzzle, all other challenges and worries can be put aside. The puzzle becomes your focus and as a result, your brain feels refreshed and ready to tackle whatever life throws at you. Other researchers are finding Sudoku as a way to slow the progress of Alzheimer's disease (Critser 2006).

This puzzle with its simple rules and small numbers can be a tool for students, teachers, and parents. For students, it helps them develop logical reasoning skills and problem-solving strategies. Students will become self-disciplined, patient, and careful problem solvers. For teachers, it is a tool for differentiating instruction, engaging students, and supporting language acquisition. For parents, it is a family pastime that reduces stress, increases focus, and turns a child from a math hater to a math lover.

Works Cited

Bennett, J. 2006. Addicted to Sudoku. An interview with Will Shortz. *Newsweek* (Society, Web Exclusive), February 23.

Critser, G. 2006. Changing minds in Alzheimer's research. *Los Angeles Times*, November 5.

Evered, L. J. 2001. Riddles, puzzles, and paradoxes. *Mathematics Teaching in the Middle School* 6 (8): 458–461.

Raizen, E. 1999. Liar or truth-teller? Logic puzzles in the foreign-language classroom. *Texas Papers in Foreign Language Education* 4 (n1): 39–50.

Sharp, J. 2006. International perspectives, beyond Su Doku. *Mathematics Teaching in the Middle School* 12 (3): 165–169.

Smullyan, R. 1982. *The Lady or the Tiger and Other Logic Puzzles*. New York: Alfred Knopf.

Learn to Play Sudoku

Sudoku Words

- **items**—the letters or numbers in the cells of the puzzle
- **mini-grid**—group of square cells that make a large square or rectangle
- **column**—line of cells that go up and down
- **row**—line of cells that go side to side
- **hints**—cells that are filled in before you start the puzzle
- **scanning**—looking at the mini-grids, columns, and rows to find cells with only one possibility for the missing item

Sudoku Rules

- Every mini-grid must have one each of each item.
- Every column must have one each of each item.
- Every row must have one each of each item.

How to Play

- **Step 1**—Look at the puzzle. Find a mini-grid that has lots of hints.
- **Step 2**—Look at each row and column. Fill in the missing items. Each item can only be once in each row or column!
- **Step 3**—Look at the columns and rows again. Check to make sure none of the items are the same. Move any that are repeated.
- **Step 4**—Repeat these steps for each mini-grid.

The Parts of a Sudoku Puzzle

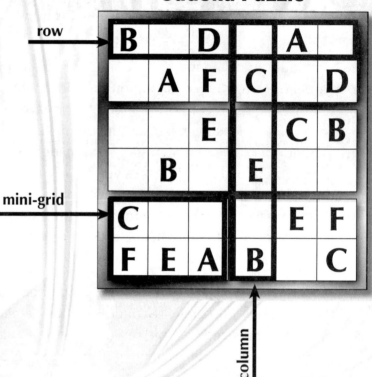

Top Secret Tip

Try this! Don't look for the mini-grid with the most hints. Look for the column or row with the most hints. Then start the puzzle there.

Strategies for Sudoku

What Is a Strategy?

A strategy is a plan, or a way to solve a puzzle. It is a good idea to have a plan when you're trying to solve math puzzles! That way, you know what steps to take as you work. Strategies definitely help you with Sudoku puzzles. Without a strategy, you may work really hard and still not be able to solve the puzzle. With a plan, you know what steps to take to work through the puzzle.

Strategy 1—Use a Puzzle Blocker

Step 1

- Cut out the Puzzle Blocker on page 63.

Step 1

Step 2

- Put the Puzzle Blocker across the puzzle.
- You want the top row to show.

Step 3

- Fill in the empty cells in the row you can see. Make sure you use a pencil because you may have to erase.
- Remove the Puzzle Blocker.

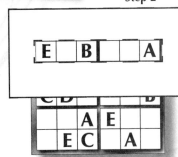

Step 2

Step 4

- Check the letters or numbers. Make sure there is only one of each in each mini-grid.
- If the items are repeated, change them in the row.

Step 5

- Turn the Puzzle Blocker and place it on the far left-hand column.
- Check the items written in the first column. Make sure there is only one of each in the column.
- If the items are repeated, change them in the column.

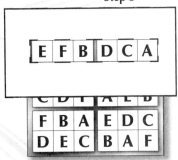

Step 3

Step 6

- Move the Puzzle Blocker to the next column and make sure no items are repeated.
- Continue to move the Puzzle Blocker over each column. Check for repeated items in each column.

Step 5

Step 7

- Place the Puzzle Blocker over the second row and fill in empty cells.
- Then repeat steps 4–6.
- After filling in the empty cells in each row, remove the puzzle blocker. Check each mini-grid, column, and row.

Strategies for Sudoku *(cont.)*

Step 1

- Find the mini-grid with the most hints. Ask, "What letters or numbers are missing from the mini-grid?"

- Write those missing items outside the mini-grid. These are the only items needed to complete this mini-grid.

- If there is only one empty cell, fill in the missing item and go to another mini-grid.

- If there is more than one empty cell, go to step 2.

Step 2

- Look at a row of the puzzle that crosses the mini-grid from step 1.

- In each empty cell, write any items that are missing in both the mini-grid and the row. Use the list you wrote outside the mini-grid.

- If there is only one possible item left for a cell, fill in the cell with that item.

- If there is more than one possible item, go to step 3.

Step 3

- Repeat step 2 for each row of the puzzle that crosses the mini-grid.

- Move onto step 4 if there are still empty cells in the mini-grid.

Step 4

- Look at a column of the puzzle that crosses the mini-grid from step 1.

- In some of the cells, there will be numbers written from steps 2–3. Cross out any items that are already given in that column.

- If there is only one possible item left for a cell, fill in the cell with that item.

- If there is more than one possible item, go to step 5.

Step 5

- Repeat step 4 for each column of the puzzle that crosses the mini-grid.

- Move onto step 6 if there are still empty cells in the mini-grid that can be filled in with more than one possible item.

Step 6

- Repeat steps 2–5 for all the other mini-grids in the puzzle.

- If you have done all this scanning and still have empty cells, you may have to make an educated guess for one cell. Then, repeat steps 2–5.

How to Use This Book

Leveled Puzzles

Beginning

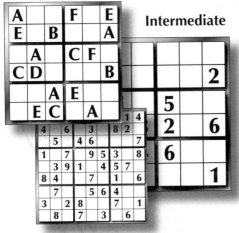

Intermediate

Challenging

- The Sudoku puzzles in this book are divided into three levels: beginning, intermediate, and challenging. Each level has a specific puzzle variation. There are 15 puzzles for each level. That makes a total of 45 puzzles in this book.

- As students move through each level, the puzzles get more difficult. When math teachers created these puzzles, they progressively decreased the number of hints within each variation. They also analyzed the difficulty of each puzzle by the types of logic needed to solve it. Puzzle solvers solved the puzzles to ensure there was one correct solution for each puzzle. In addition, each level of *Learn & Play: Sudoku* was field tested in classrooms.

Themes of Puzzles

- Each of the three levels has a content-area theme tied to state and national standards. The beginning puzzles have a science theme. The intermediate puzzles have a math theme, and the challenging puzzles have a social studies theme.

- All the math themes are tied to the Curriculum Focal Points as identified by the National Council of Teachers of Mathematics.

- Throughout each section, the titles, images, and captions relate to the theme.

Special Additions

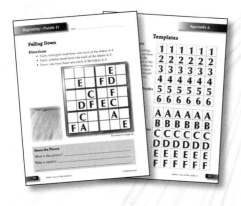

- Special additions are included within each section of puzzles. Some pages have fun facts related to the images. On other pages, students get to write their own fun facts. The last five puzzles in each section show close-ups of pictures. Students should guess what the picture is and write a new caption.

- The appendices include templates, a list of photograph sources, and the answer key. The answer key shows the completed puzzles for your reference.

Introduction

Puzzle Variations at Each Grade Level

	Easy or Beginner		Medium or Intermediate		Hard or Challenging	
	Variation	Hints	Variation	Hints	Variation	Hints
First Grade	1 x 1 with pictures	3–1	2 x 2 with pictures	11–8	2 x 2 with numbers	8–5
Second Grade	2 x 2 with pictures	11–8	2 x 2 with numbers	7–5	2 x 2 with letters	6–4
Third Grade	2 x 2 with pictures	6–4	2 x 3 with letters	20–18	2 x 3 with numbers	17–14
Fourth Grade	2 x 3 with letters	17–15	2 x 3 with numbers	15–13	3 x 3 with numbers	44–40
Fifth Grade	2 x 3 with numbers	12–10	3 x 3 with letters	40–36	3 x 3 with numbers	36–32

Correlations

The activities in this book meet the following standards:

- Students understand and apply basic principles of logic and reasoning.
- Students effectively use mental processes that are based on identifying similarities and differences.
- Students apply basic trouble-shooting and problem-solving techniques.
- Students apply effective decision-making techniques.
- Students use trial and error and the process of elimination to solve problems.

Copyright 2004 McREL. www.mcrel.org/standards-benchmarks.

A correlation of these standards for your state can be printed directly from the Shell Education website: **http://www.shelleducation.com**. If you require assistance in printing correlation reports, please contact Customer Service at 1-800-877-3450.

Landforms

Name _____

What a Jump!

Directions

- Every mini-grid must have one each of the letters A–F.
- Every column must have one each of the letters A–F.
- Every row must have one each of the letters A–F.

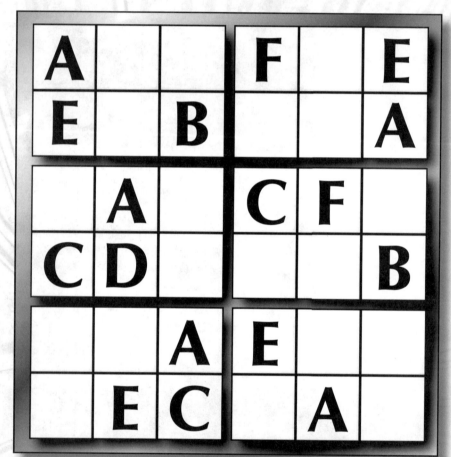

The answer is on page 65.

Over 100 years ago, this person jumped between two canyon ledges at the Grand Canyon.

#50323—*Learn & Play: Sudoku 4* © *Shell Education*

Landforms

Name _____

What a Jump!

Directions

- Every mini-grid must have one each of the letters A–F.
- Every column must have one each of the letters A–F.
- Every row must have one each of the letters A–F.

A			F		E
E		B			A
	A		C	F	
C	D				B
		A	E		
	E	C		A	

The answer is on page 65.

Over 100 years ago, this person jumped between two canyon ledges at the Grand Canyon.

#50323—Learn & Play: Sudoku 4

Name _____

Sheer Drop

Directions

- Every mini-grid must have one each of the letters A–F.
- Every column must have one each of the letters A–F.
- Every row must have one each of the letters A–F.

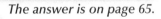
The answer is on page 65.

Half Dome is probably Yosemite's most familiar sight.

Name _____

Sand Storm

Directions

- Every mini-grid must have one each of the letters A–F.
- Every column must have one each of the letters A–F.
- Every row must have one each of the letters A–F.

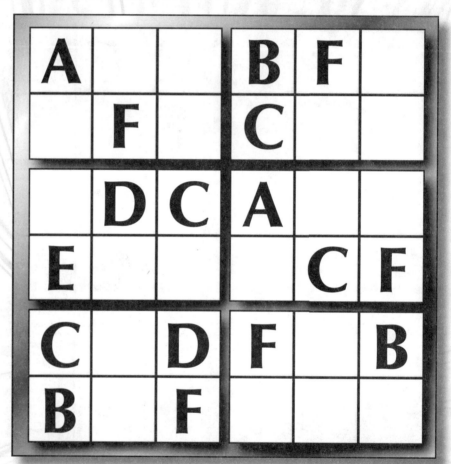

The answer is on page 65.

This sand dune is so
perfect, it doesn't look real.

Name _____

Freezing Cold

Directions

- Every mini-grid must have one each of the letters A–F.
- Every column must have one each of the letters A–F.
- Every row must have one each of the letters A–F.

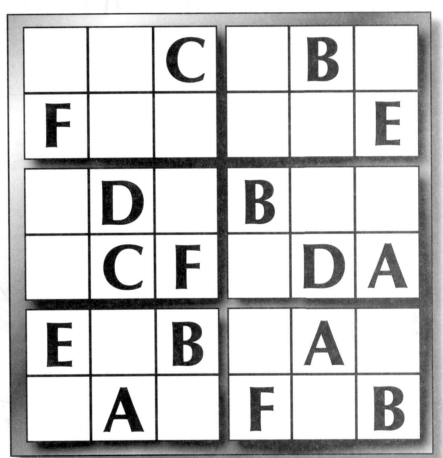

The answer is on page 65.

Tundras are huge treeless plains in the arctic.

Name _____

Standing Tall

Directions

- Every mini-grid must have one each of the letters A–F.
- Every column must have one each of the letters A–F.
- Every row must have one each of the letters A–F.

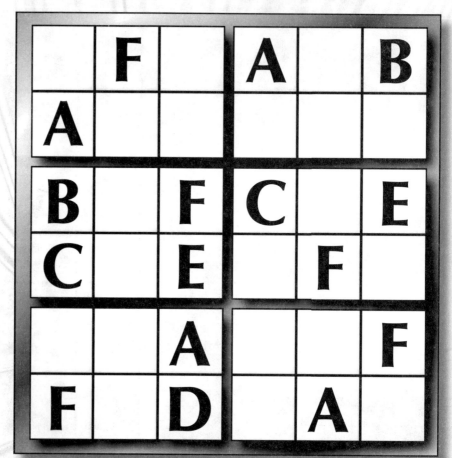

The answer is on page 65.

A butte is an isolated hill or mountain.

Name _____

Meandering Along

Directions

- Every mini-grid must have one each of the letters A–F.
- Every column must have one each of the letters A–F.
- Every row must have one each of the letters A–F.

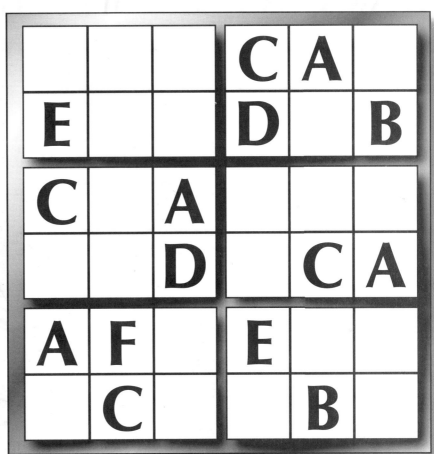

The Grand Canyon runs for 277 miles.

The answer is on page 65.

The Colorado River is over a mile below the edge of the Grand Canyon at some spots.

Name _____

Prickly to the Touch

Directions

- Every mini-grid must have one each of the letters A–F.
- Every column must have one each of the letters A–F.
- Every row must have one each of the letters A–F.

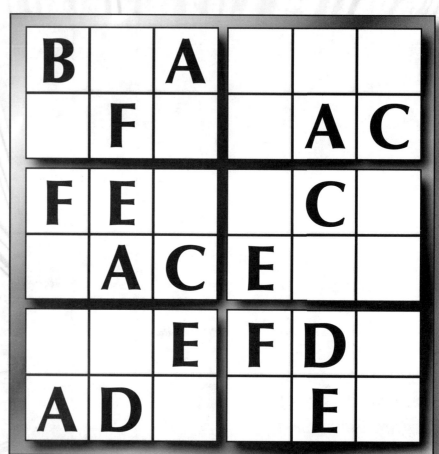

Saguaros are cactuses that thrive in Arizona's desert.

The answer is on page 66.

Write your own fun fact:_____

_____

Name _____

Keep Your Balance

Directions

- Every mini-grid must have one each of the letters A–F.
- Every column must have one each of the letters A–F.
- Every row must have one each of the letters A–F.

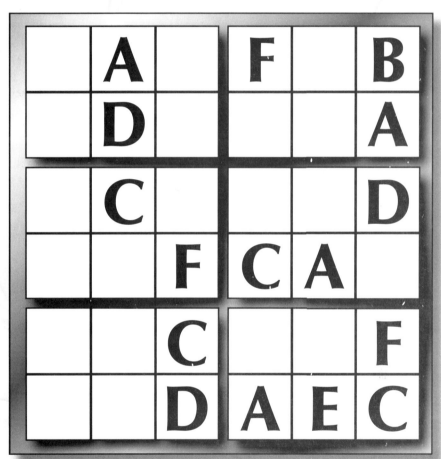

High-wire tightrope acts used to be performed over Niagara Falls.

The answer is on page 66.

The first person to go over Niagara Falls and survive was a 63-year-old female teacher.

Name _____

Rolling On . . .

Directions

- Every mini-grid must have one each of the letters A–F.
- Every column must have one each of the letters A–F.
- Every row must have one each of the letters A–F.

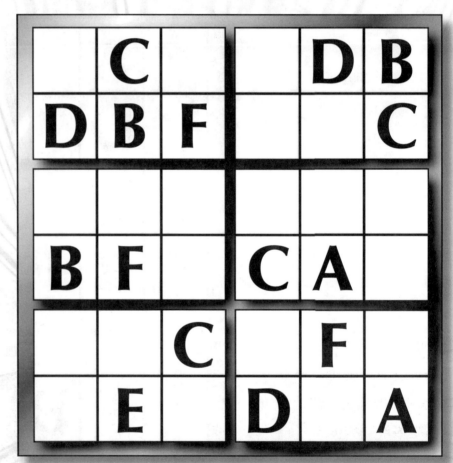

Plains are stretches of land that change little in elevation.

The answer is on page 66.

Write your own fun fact:_____

_____

Name _____

Bird Watering Hole

Directions

- Every mini-grid must have one each of the letters A–F.
- Every column must have one each of the letters A–F.
- Every row must have one each of the letters A–F.

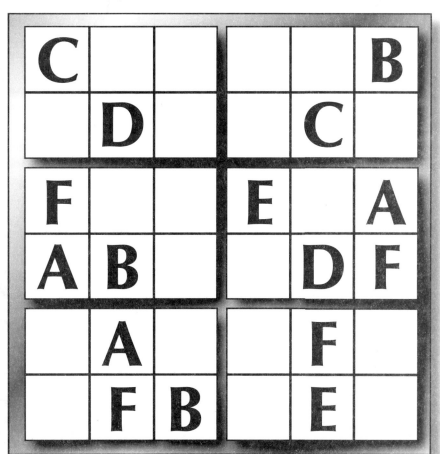

Migrating birds often stop at wetlands for drinks of water.

The answer is on page 66.

Some wetlands only have water during the rainy spring season. They are dry for the rest of the year.

Name _____

Falling Down

Directions

- Every mini-grid must have one each of the letters A–F.
- Every column must have one each of the letters A–F.
- Every row must have one each of the letters A–F.

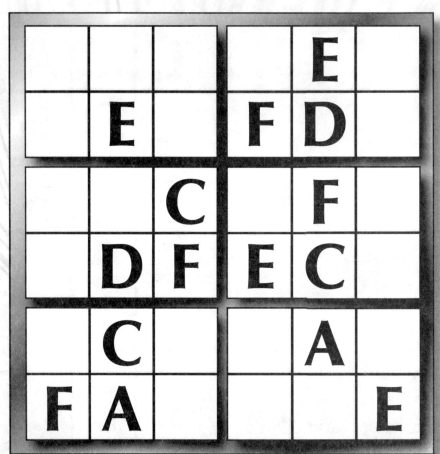

The answer is on page 66.

Guess the Picture

What is this picture? _____

Write a caption: _____

_____

Name _____

Hard Edges

Directions

- Every mini-grid must have one each of the letters A–F.
- Every column must have one each of the letters A–F.
- Every row must have one each of the letters A–F.

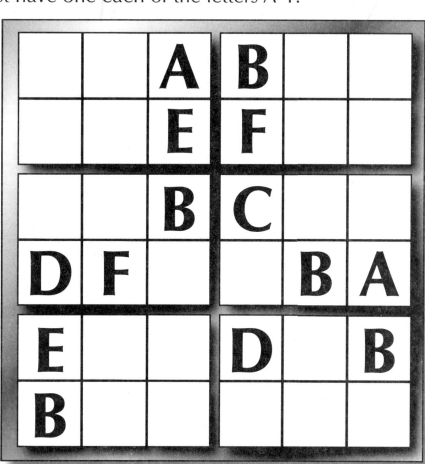

The answer is on page 66.

Guess the Picture

What is this picture? _____

Write a caption: _____

_____

Name _____

Sandy Walk

Directions

- Every mini-grid must have one each of the letters A–F.
- Every column must have one each of the letters A–F.
- Every row must have one each of the letters A–F.

The answer is on page 67.

Guess the Picture

What is this picture? _____

Write a caption: _____

_____

Name _____

Water Fountain

Directions

- Every mini-grid must have one each of the letters A–F.
- Every column must have one each of the letters A–F.
- Every row must have one each of the letters A–F.

The answer is on page 67.

Guess the Picture

What is this picture? _____

Write a caption: _____

_____

Name _____

Close Quarters

Directions

- Every mini-grid must have one each of the letters A–F.
- Every column must have one each of the letters A–F.
- Every row must have one each of the letters A–F.

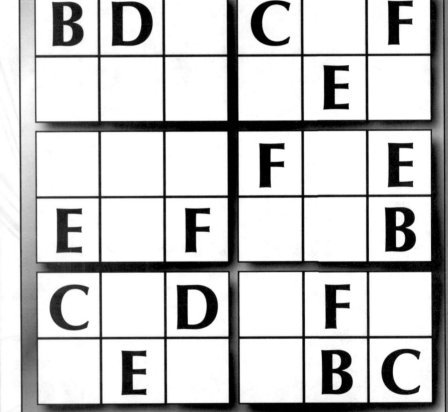

The answer is on page 67.

Guess the Picture

What is this picture? _____

Write a caption: _____

_____

Decimals

Counting Your Pennies

Directions

- Every mini-grid must have one each of the numbers 1–6.
- Every column must have one each of the numbers 1–6.
- Every row must have one each of the numbers 1–6.

3					
6					2
	1		5		
		3	2		6
1		4	6		
					4

The answer is on page 67.

These dollar bills and coins
equal $35.68.

Portion Control

Directions

- Every mini-grid must have one each of the numbers 1–6.
- Every column must have one each of the numbers 1–6.
- Every row must have one each of the numbers 1–6.

6		3			1
			4		6
2		5			
3					2
	2			6	5
	3			2	

The answer is on page 67.

Kitchen scales give digital readouts of food's weight.

Name _____

Exact Time

Directions

- Every mini-grid must have one each of the numbers 1–6.
- Every column must have one each of the numbers 1–6.
- Every row must have one each of the numbers 1–6.

		6		3	2
5		2	4		6
3			6		
	6				5
1			2		
6		4			3

The answer is on page 67.

Digital stopwatches are accurate to a hundredth of a second.

Name _____

On Your Way

Directions

- Every mini-grid must have one each of the numbers 1–6.
- Every column must have one each of the numbers 1–6.
- Every row must have one each of the numbers 1–6.

5			3		
		2		4	
4	2				
	1		2		4
1		6		2	3
				5	6

The answer is on page 68.

This odometer tracks the total distance the car has traveled in tenths of kilometers.

Name _____

What a Bargain!

Directions

- Every mini-grid must have one each of the numbers 1–6.
- Every column must have one each of the numbers 1–6.
- Every row must have one each of the numbers 1–6.

5			6		3
2	5			1	
1	4			6	2
4			1		
3			2		

The answer is on page 68.

Receipts use a decimal system to show what money was spent.

Name _____

Feeling Sick?

Directions

- Every mini-grid must have one each of the numbers 1–6.
- Every column must have one each of the numbers 1–6.
- Every row must have one each of the numbers 1–6.

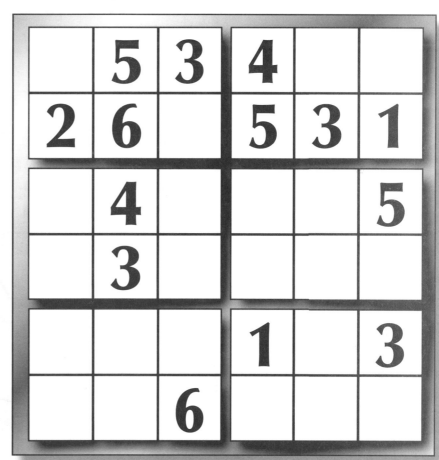

Some medical thermometers give a digital temperature reading.

The answer is on page 68.

Write your own fun fact: _____

_____

Name _____

Weighing In

Directions

- Every mini-grid must have one each of the numbers 1–6.
- Every column must have one each of the numbers 1–6.
- Every row must have one each of the numbers 1–6.

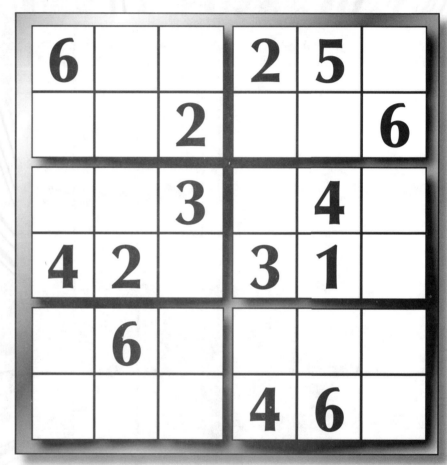

On a digital scale, this man weighs 83.4 kilograms. That is 184 pounds.

The answer is on page 68.

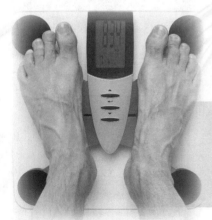

Write your own fun fact: _____

_____

What's the Total?

Directions

- Every mini-grid must have one each of the numbers 1–6.
- Every column must have one each of the numbers 1–6.
- Every row must have one each of the numbers 1–6.

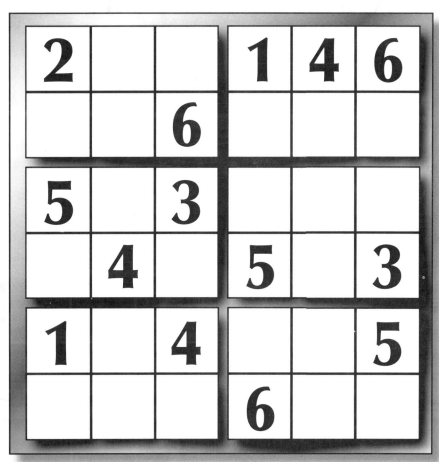

Calculators use a decimal system.

The answer is on page 68.

Abacuses are sometimes called the first calculators. An abacus was usually on a wooden frame with beads that slide on wires.

Play the Music

Directions

- Every mini-grid must have one each of the numbers 1–6.
- Every column must have one each of the numbers 1–6.
- Every row must have one each of the numbers 1–6.

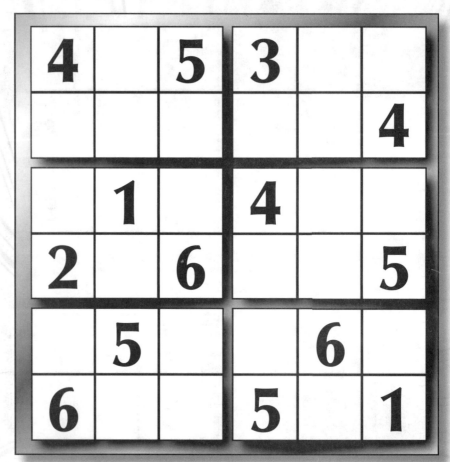

Radios with digital systems are best for tuning into stations.

The answer is on page 68.

There are about 13,500 radio stations that broadcast in the United States.

Name _____

And the Total Is . . .

Directions

- Every mini-grid must have one each of the numbers 1–6.
- Every column must have one each of the numbers 1–6.
- Every row must have one each of the numbers 1–6.

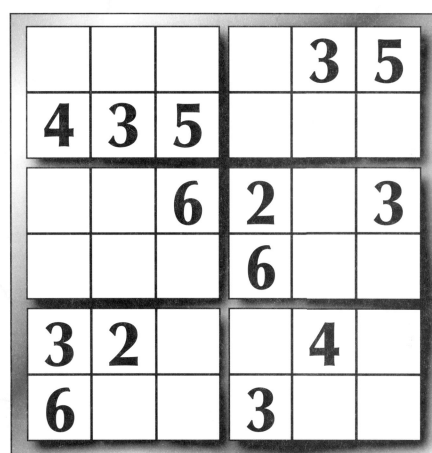

Cash registers tally our purchases.

The answer is on page 69.

The cash register was invented in 1879 to stop employees from stealing money.

Name _____

Too Heavy?

Directions

- Every mini-grid must have one each of the numbers 1–6.
- Every column must have one each of the numbers 1–6.
- Every row must have one each of the numbers 1–6.

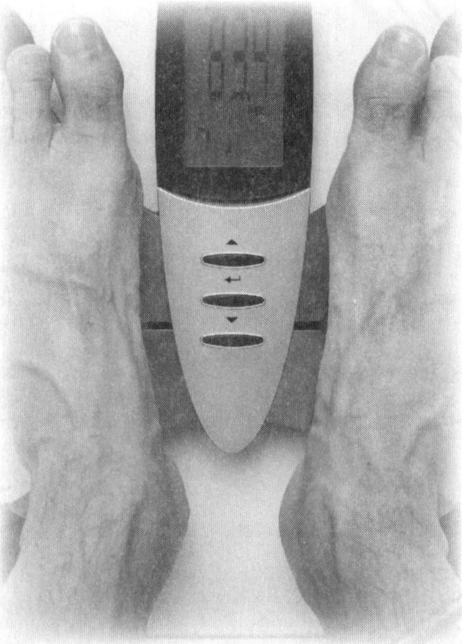

1				5	
		5	1		4
3		4	6		
				4		1
	6	1			3

The answer is on page 69.

Guess the Picture

What is this picture? _____

Write a caption: _____

_____

Name _____

Add It Up

Directions

- Every mini-grid must have one each of the numbers 1–6.
- Every column must have one each of the numbers 1–6.
- Every row must have one each of the numbers 1–6.

	4	6		5	
	2			4	
4				3	
	3	2	5	6	
		4	1		

The answer is on page 69.

Guess the Picture

What is this picture? _____

Write a caption: _____

_____

Name _____

Run Fast

Directions

- Every mini-grid must have one each of the numbers 1–6.
- Every column must have one each of the numbers 1–6.
- Every row must have one each of the numbers 1–6.

		2	1		
6				4	2
5		6			
3		4		6	
			2		
				1	5

The answer is on page 69.

Guess the Picture

What is this picture? _____

Write a caption: _____

_____

Name _____

Tune It In

Directions

- Every mini-grid must have one each of the numbers 1–6.
- Every column must have one each of the numbers 1–6.
- Every row must have one each of the numbers 1–6.

		3	2		
	6				5
	3			5	
1					6
	4			2	
2			6		3

The answer is on page 69.

Guess the Picture

What is this picture? _____

Write a caption: _____

_____

Name _____

Ring It Up

Directions

- Every mini-grid must have one each of the numbers 1–6.
- Every column must have one each of the numbers 1–6.
- Every row must have one each of the numbers 1–6.

3	2		4		
4				1	
	4				6
6				4	
		6		5	
2					

The answer is on page 69.

Guess the Picture

What is this picture? _____

Write a caption: _____

_____

American Indians

One-Room Home

Directions

- Every mini-grid must have one each of the numbers 1–9.
- Every column must have one each of the numbers 1–9.
- Every row must have one each of the numbers 1–9.

	9		5		8		1	4
4		6		3		8	2	
	5		4	6				7
1		7		9	5	3		8
	3	9	1		4	5	7	
8	4			7			1	6
	7			5	6	4		
3		2	8				7	1
	8		7		3		6	

The answer is on page 70.

Some American Indian tribes lived in tepees.

#50323—Learn & Play: Sudoku 4

Name _____

Beautiful Baskets

Directions

- Every mini-grid must have one each of the numbers 1–9.
- Every column must have one each of the numbers 1–9.
- Every row must have one each of the numbers 1–9.

3			8		4	5	2	
	5	8		7				6
6		2			3	8	1	
	9		2	4			6	
7	1		6			2		3
2		5		1	9		7	8
4	2		5			7		1
	8		4	9	1		3	
1		6		2	8			4

The answer is on page 70.

American Indians weave
beautiful, leak-proof
baskets.

Name _____

Arrowheads

Directions

- Every mini-grid must have one each of the numbers 1–9.
- Every column must have one each of the numbers 1–9.
- Every row must have one each of the numbers 1–9.

7		6		1		2		3
		4	3		7		6	
3	5			9	6	8		4
6	7			2		3		9
		5	6		1		2	
4	1	2		7		6		5
2			1	6			3	
	8	3			2	1		6
1	6		8	3		7		

The answer is on page 70.

Early American Indians used arrows for hunting and fighting.

#50323—*Learn & Play: Sudoku 4*   © *Shell Education*

Name _____

Music Maker

Directions

- Every mini-grid must have one each of the numbers 1–9.
- Every column must have one each of the numbers 1–9.
- Every row must have one each of the numbers 1–9.

9	7	3		4		6	5	2
			5		3	4		7
6	4		2	9			1	
2		6		7	9		8	
	9	4				7		1
		7	1	8				9
	3		6		8		2	4
5		2		1		9		6
4	6		9		2	5	7	

The answer is on page 70.

Kokopelli was first drawn over 2,000 years ago in petroglyphs.

Name _____

All Dressed Up

Directions

- Every mini-grid must have one each of the numbers 1–9.
- Every column must have one each of the numbers 1–9.
- Every row must have one each of the numbers 1–9.

3		5		9	8		7	
	2					4	1	
8	1		2	4	6	3		
2		3				9		1
	6		9		1		4	
	9	4	8	3		7	6	2
9				5	4	1	3	
	3	1	7			6		9
	7	6		1	9		2	

The answer is on page 70.

An American Indian,
wearing traditional dress,
is dancing at a powwow.

Name _____

Don't Look Down!

Directions

- Every mini-grid must have one each of the numbers 1–9.
- Every column must have one each of the numbers 1–9.
- Every row must have one each of the numbers 1–9.

6		2		8	9		5	7
	9		1		3	8		
	8			7		1	2	
4	3			5	8			1
		1	9	3	4			
9	5	8				4	7	3
7			5		2		6	8
	6	9	3	4				
	2			9		7		4

Long ago, American Indians built homes into the sides of mountains.

The answer is on page 70.

The ancient Puebloans first built homes on the mesa tops and the cliff sides over 2,500 years ago.

Name _____

Colorful Clay

Directions

- Every mini-grid must have one each of the numbers 1–9.
- Every column must have one each of the numbers 1–9.
- Every row must have one each of the numbers 1–9.

	1		9	8		7		5
3			1		2			
4	8			7		1	6	2
		1	4		8		7	
7		2				9	8	3
	6		2	9			4	
1		7	8		6			9
6				1		3	2	8
	2	8	3		5			7

Outdoor markets often sell pottery made by American Indians.

The answer is on page 71.

Write your own fun fact: _____

_____

#50323—Learn & Play: Sudoku 4   © *Shell Education*

Name _____

Rocky Pictures

Directions

- Every mini-grid must have one each of the numbers 1–9.
- Every column must have one each of the numbers 1–9.
- Every row must have one each of the numbers 1–9.

8	1			2	3		6	
3					8			5
	5		7		6	3	1	
	7			6	4		5	9
4		2	3		9		7	
	6		8	7			3	2
	2			3		5		1
5	3	4	1		2			
	9		6	8		2		3

Petroglyphs are rock carvings drawn by early American Indians.

The answer is on page 71.

Write your own fun fact: _____

_____

Name _____

Millions of Bison

Directions

- Every mini-grid must have one each of the numbers 1–9.
- Every column must have one each of the numbers 1–9.
- Every row must have one each of the numbers 1–9.

	9	1	7					4
8			3		2			5
	6	3	9			7	1	
4		7	6	2	3			1
				4		3		6
3		6	1	9	7	4		
	3		4		9		8	
	1		8		6			
9		8	2		1	6	5	3

Plains Indians hunted bison for thousands of years.

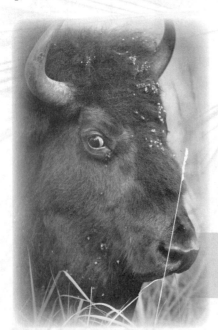

The answer is on page 71.

When early explorers landed in America, up to 60 million bison roamed throughout the land.

Name _____

Standing Straight

Directions

- Every mini-grid must have one each of the numbers 1–9.
- Every column must have one each of the numbers 1–9.
- Every row must have one each of the numbers 1–9.

		1	2		7	4		
4			8		1		6	2
2	5			9			8	1
	7	5			8	6	1	
1	8	2				5	3	
	4			7			9	
5	1			8	2			3
7			5		3			6
	2	8	9		6	1	7	

Indians in the Pacific Northwest create art from giant trees.

The answer is on page 71.

Totem poles are carved by American Indians to tell stories about their families or important legends.

Northwestern Indians

Directions

- Every mini-grid must have one each of the numbers 1–9.
- Every column must have one each of the numbers 1–9.
- Every row must have one each of the numbers 1–9.

	1		5			8	4	
2		4		6	8	1		5
	8	6	1				2	
3		2				4		7
	4		7	5	9			
6		7		2		5		1
	6		3		7		1	
8		3		9		7		4
4			2		5			3

The answer is on page 71.

Guess the Picture

What is this picture? _____

Write a caption: _____

_____

Name _____

Animal Images

Directions

- Every mini-grid must have one each of the numbers 1–9.
- Every column must have one each of the numbers 1–9.
- Every row must have one each of the numbers 1–9.

		2	5		6			
4		8				6		7
	7		8		1		2	
9		3		8		1		4
			3		9			5
7		1		6	5	8		9
	3		1		8		4	
1		4	2			3		8
	8		6		4		1	

The answer is on page 71.

Guess the Picture

What is this picture? _____

Write a caption: _____

_____

Name _____

Powwow

Directions

- Every mini-grid must have one each of the numbers 1–9.
- Every column must have one each of the numbers 1–9.
- Every row must have one each of the numbers 1–9.

	6		7		1	3	4	
7		9		3			1	
	1			4		7		6
				9	4	1		3
	5	6			3	9		4
9	3			2	6		8	
		1			2	4		
4			3	1				8
6		7		5		2	3	1

The answer is on page 72.

Guess the Picture

What is this picture? _____

Write a caption: _____

_____

Name _____

Roaming Spirit

Directions

- Every mini-grid must have one each of the numbers 1–9.
- Every column must have one each of the numbers 1–9.
- Every row must have one each of the numbers 1–9.

	4		3	1			7	
2	1		7				8	
	3		4		2		6	
			8	6	3			2
9	8	2				3	1	
3			2	9	1			
		8	1					5
1				7	5		4	8
5	9			2	8	1	3	7

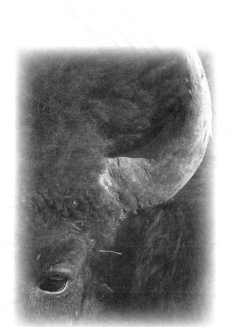

The answer is on page 72.

Guess the Picture

What is this picture? _____

Write a caption: _____

_____

Name _____

Painted Vessel

Directions

- Every mini-grid must have one each of the numbers 1–9.
- Every column must have one each of the numbers 1–9.
- Every row must have one each of the numbers 1–9.

2	7		4	8				1
		9			1	4		8
	8			5		2	7	
8					5	1		
3		2	8			5		
	4	6	2	1				9
	2		1	7	3		4	5
4	3					7		2
	6	5	9		2		1	

The answer is on page 72.

Guess the Picture

What is this picture? _____

Write a caption: _____

_____

#50323—*Learn & Play: Sudoku 4*   © *Shell Education*

Templates

Number Cut Outs

Directions: Instead of writing the numbers in pencil, use these cutout numbers to fill in the puzzle. Cut out the boxes on the dotted lines. Then place them in the puzzle. You can then move them around on the puzzle until you find all the right spaces!

Beginning Puzzles

1	1	1	1	1	1
2	2	2	2	2	2
3	3	3	3	3	3
4	4	4	4	4	4
5	5	5	5	5	5
6	6	6	6	6	6

Letter Cut Outs

Intermediate Puzzles

A	A	A	A	A	A
B	B	B	B	B	B
C	C	C	C	C	C
D	D	D	D	D	D
E	E	E	E	E	E
F	F	F	F	F	F

Templates *(cont.)*

Number Cut Outs

Challenging Puzzles

1	1	1	1	1	1	1	1	1
2	2	2	2	2	2	2	2	2
3	3	3	3	3	3	3	3	3
4	4	4	4	4	4	4	4	4
5	5	5	5	5	5	5	5	5
6	6	6	6	6	6	6	6	6
7	7	7	7	7	7	7	7	7
8	8	8	8	8	8	8	8	8
9	9	9	9	9	9	9	9	9

Templates *(cont.)*

Puzzle Blockers

Directions: Cut out the rectangle. Then make a window by cutting along the dotted line.

For Beginning and Intermediate Puzzles

Cut out this part.

For Challenging Puzzles

Cut out this part.

Photograph Sources

Page	Puzzle Title	Photograph Source
14	What a Jump!	ChipPix/Shutterstock, Inc.
15	Sheer Drop	Julie Fine/Shutterstock, Inc.
16	Sand Storm	Vova Pomortzeff/Shutterstock, Inc.
17	Freezing Cold	Socrates/Shutterstock, Inc.
18	Standing Tall	Albo/Shutterstock, Inc.
19	Meandering Along	Oksana Perkins/Shutterstock, Inc.
20	Prickly to the Touch	Nelson Sirlin/Shutterstock, Inc.
21	Keep Your Balance	Bryan Busovicki/Shutterstock, Inc.
22	Rolling On . . .	L. Renault/Shutterstock, Inc.
23	Bird Watering Hole	Peter Blottman/Shutterstock, Inc.
24	Falling Down	Bryan Busovicki/Shutterstock, Inc.
25	Hard Edges	Julie Fine/Shutterstock, Inc.
26	Sandy Walk	Elena Ray/Shutterstock, Inc.
27	Water Fountain	Serg64/Shutterstock, Inc.
28	Close Quarters	Galyna Andrushko/Shutterstock, Inc.
30	Counting Your Pennies	Absolut/Shutterstock, Inc.
31	Portion Control	Oktay Ortakcioglu/Shutterstock, Inc.
32	Exact Time	PLS/Shutterstock, Inc.
33	On Your Way	Titus Manea/Shutterstock, Inc.
34	What a Bargain!	Olga Lis/Shutterstock, Inc.
35	Feeling Sick?	Tom Davison/Shutterstock, Inc.
36	Weighing In	Kameel4u/Shutterstock, Inc.
37	What's the Total?	Thorsten Rust/Shutterstock, Inc.
38	Play the Music	Tim Tran/Shutterstock, Inc.
39	And the Total Is . . .	Natalia Bratslavsky/Shutterstock, Inc.
40	Too Heavy?	Kameel4u/Shutterstock, Inc.
41	Add It Up	Thorsten Rust/Shutterstock, Inc.
42	Run Fast	VisualField/Shutterstock, Inc.
43	Tune It In	Univega/Shutterstock, Inc.
44	Ring It Up	Billy Lobo H./Shutterstock, Inc.
46	One-Room Home	Kurt De Bruyn/Shutterstock, Inc.
47	Beautiful Baskets	Michael LeDray/Shutterstock, Inc.
48	Arrowheads	LH/Shutterstock, Inc.
49	Music Maker	Siege/Shutterstock, Inc.
50	All Dressed Up	Piotr Przeszlo/Shutterstock, Inc.
51	Don't Look Down!	John S. Sfondilias/Shutterstock, Inc.
52	Colorful Clay	Douglas Knight/Shutterstock, Inc.
53	Rocky Pictures	Mike Norton/Shutterstock, Inc.
54	Millions of Bison	Vasily A. Ilyinsky/Shutterstock, Inc.
55	Standing Straight	Ryan Morgan/Shutterstock, Inc.
56	Northwestern Indians	Ryan Morgan/Shutterstock, Inc.
57	Animal Images	Mike Norton/Shutterstock, Inc.
58	Powwow	Jim Parkin/Shutterstock, Inc.
59	Roaming Spirit	Sebastien Burel/Shutterstock, Inc.
60	Painted Vessel	Aiyana Paterson-Zinkand/Shutterstock, Inc.

Answer Key

What a Jump! (page 14)

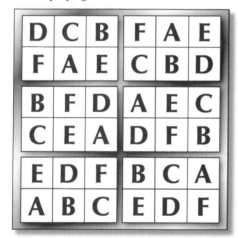

Sheer Drop (page 15)

Sand Storm (page 16)

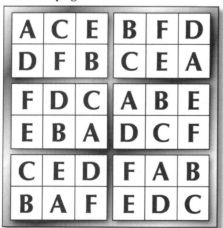

Freezing Cold (page 17)

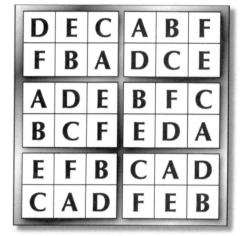

Standing Tall (page 18)

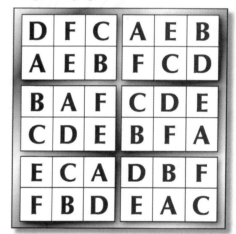

Meandering Along (page 19)

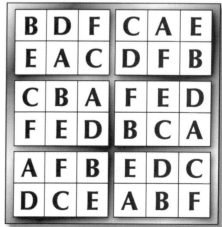

Answer Key *(cont.)*

Prickly to the Touch (page 20)

B	C	A	D	F	E
E	F	D	B	A	C
F	E	B	A	C	D
D	A	C	E	B	F
C	B	E	F	D	A
A	D	F	C	E	B

Keep Your Balance (page 21)

C	A	E	F	D	B
F	D	B	E	C	A
E	C	A	B	F	D
D	B	F	C	A	E
A	E	C	D	B	F
B	F	D	A	E	C

Rolling On . . . (page 22)

E	C	A	F	D	B
D	B	F	A	E	C
C	A	D	E	B	F
B	F	E	C	A	D
A	D	C	B	F	E
F	E	B	D	C	A

Bird Watering Hole (page 23)

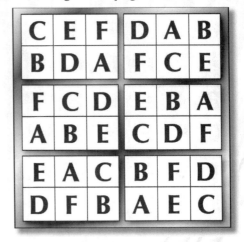

C	E	F	D	A	B
B	D	A	F	C	E
F	C	D	E	B	A
A	B	E	C	D	F
E	A	C	B	F	D
D	F	B	A	E	C

Falling Down (page 24)

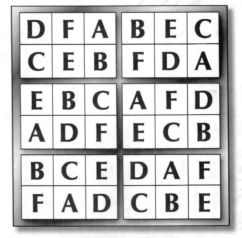

D	F	A	B	E	C
C	E	B	F	D	A
E	B	C	A	F	D
A	D	F	E	C	B
B	C	E	D	A	F
F	A	D	C	B	E

Hard Edges (page 25)

F	D	A	B	E	C
C	B	E	F	A	D
A	E	B	C	D	F
D	F	C	E	B	A
E	A	F	D	C	B
B	C	D	A	F	E

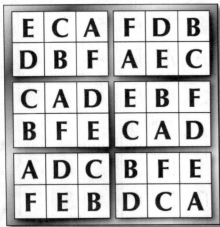

Answer Key *(cont.)*

Sandy Walk (page 26)

C	E	D	F	B	A
A	B	F	D	E	C
B	A	E	C	D	F
D	F	C	E	A	B
F	D	A	B	C	E
E	C	B	A	F	D

Water Fountain (page 27)

A	E	B	C	D	F
D	F	C	B	E	A
B	A	E	D	F	C
C	D	F	A	B	E
F	C	D	E	A	B
E	B	A	F	C	D

Close Quarters (page 28)

B	D	E	C	A	F
A	F	C	B	E	D
D	A	B	F	C	E
E	C	F	A	D	B
C	B	D	E	F	A
F	E	A	D	B	C

Counting Your Pennies (page 30)

3	2	5	4	6	1
6	4	1	3	5	2
2	1	6	5	4	3
4	5	3	2	1	6
1	3	4	6	2	5
5	6	2	1	3	4

Portion Control (page 31)

6	4	3	2	5	1
1	5	2	4	3	6
2	1	5	6	4	3
3	6	4	5	1	2
4	2	1	3	6	5
5	3	6	1	2	4

Exact Time (page 32)

4	1	6	5	3	2
5	3	2	4	1	6
3	4	5	6	2	1
2	6	1	3	4	5
1	5	3	2	6	4
6	2	4	1	5	3

Answer Key *(cont.)*

On Your Way (page 33)

5	4	1	3	6	2
3	6	2	5	4	1
4	2	3	6	1	5
6	1	5	2	3	4
1	5	6	4	2	3
2	3	4	1	5	6

Weighing In (page 36)

6	3	1	2	5	4
5	4	2	1	3	6
1	5	3	6	4	2
4	2	6	3	1	5
3	6	4	5	2	1
2	1	5	4	6	3

What a Bargain! (page 34)

6	3	2	4	5	1
5	1	4	6	2	3
2	5	6	3	1	4
1	4	3	5	6	2
4	2	5	1	3	6
3	6	1	2	4	5

What's the Total? (page 37)

2	3	5	1	4	6
4	1	6	3	5	2
5	2	3	4	6	1
6	4	1	5	2	3
1	6	4	2	3	5
3	5	2	6	1	4

Feeling Sick? (page 35)

1	5	3	4	2	6
2	6	4	5	3	1
6	4	2	3	1	5
5	3	1	6	4	2
4	2	5	1	6	3
3	1	6	2	5	4

Play the Music (page 38)

4	6	5	3	1	2
3	2	1	6	5	4
5	1	3	4	2	6
2	4	6	1	3	5
1	5	4	2	6	3
6	3	2	5	4	1

Answer Key *(cont.)*

And the Total Is . . . (page 39)

1	6	2	4	3	5
4	3	5	1	6	2
5	4	6	2	1	3
2	1	3	6	5	4
3	2	1	5	4	6
6	5	4	3	2	1

Too Heavy? (page 40)

1	4	3	2	5	6
6	2	5	1	3	4
3	5	4	6	1	2
2	1	6	3	4	5
5	3	2	4	6	1
4	6	1	5	2	3

Add It Up (page 41)

3	4	6	2	5	1
5	2	1	3	4	6
2	6	3	4	1	5
4	1	5	6	3	2
1	3	2	5	6	4
6	5	4	1	2	3

Run Fast (page 42)

4	3	2	1	5	6
6	5	1	3	4	2
5	1	6	4	2	3
3	2	4	5	6	1
1	6	5	2	3	4
2	4	3	6	1	5

Tune It In (page 43)

5	1	3	2	6	4
4	6	2	3	1	5
6	3	4	1	5	2
1	2	5	4	3	6
3	4	6	5	2	1
2	5	1	6	4	3

Ring It Up (page 44)

3	2	1	4	6	5
4	6	5	3	1	2
5	4	3	1	2	6
6	1	2	5	4	3
1	3	6	2	5	4
2	5	4	6	3	1

Answer Key (cont.)

One-Room Home (page 46)

7	9	3	5	2	8	6	1	4
4	1	6	9	3	7	8	2	5
2	5	8	4	6	1	9	3	7
1	2	7	6	9	5	3	4	8
6	3	9	1	8	4	5	7	2
8	4	5	3	7	2	1	9	6
9	7	1	2	5	6	4	8	3
3	6	2	8	4	9	7	5	1
5	8	4	7	1	3	2	6	9

Music Maker (page 49)

9	7	3	8	4	1	6	5	2
1	2	8	5	6	3	4	9	7
6	4	5	2	9	7	8	1	3
2	1	6	4	7	9	3	8	5
8	9	4	3	2	5	7	6	1
3	5	7	1	8	6	2	4	9
7	3	9	6	5	8	1	2	4
5	8	2	7	1	4	9	3	6
4	6	1	9	3	2	5	7	8

Beautiful Baskets (page 47)

3	7	1	8	6	4	5	2	9
9	5	8	1	7	2	3	4	6
6	4	2	9	5	3	8	1	7
8	9	3	2	4	7	1	6	5
7	1	4	6	8	5	2	9	3
2	6	5	3	1	9	4	7	8
4	2	9	5	3	6	7	8	1
5	8	7	4	9	1	6	3	2
1	3	6	7	2	8	9	5	4

All Dressed Up (page 50)

3	4	5	1	9	8	2	7	6
6	2	9	5	7	3	4	1	8
8	1	7	2	4	6	3	9	5
2	5	3	4	6	7	9	8	1
7	6	8	9	2	1	5	4	3
1	9	4	8	3	5	7	6	2
9	8	2	6	5	4	1	3	7
4	3	1	7	8	2	6	5	9
5	7	6	3	1	9	8	2	4

Arrowheads (page 48)

7	9	6	4	1	8	2	5	3
8	2	4	3	5	7	9	6	1
3	5	1	2	9	6	8	7	4
6	7	8	5	2	4	3	1	9
9	3	5	6	8	1	4	2	7
4	1	2	9	7	3	6	8	5
2	4	7	1	6	9	5	3	8
5	8	3	7	4	2	1	9	6
1	6	9	8	3	5	7	4	2

Don't Look Down! (page 51)

6	1	2	4	8	9	3	5	7
5	9	7	1	2	3	8	4	6
3	8	4	6	7	5	1	2	9
4	3	6	7	5	8	2	9	1
2	7	1	9	3	4	6	8	5
9	5	8	2	6	1	4	7	3
7	4	3	5	1	2	9	6	8
8	6	9	3	4	7	5	1	2
1	2	5	8	9	6	7	3	4

Answer Key *(cont.)*

Colorful Clay (page 52)

2	1	6	9	8	4	7	3	5
3	7	5	1	6	2	8	9	4
4	8	9	5	7	3	1	6	2
5	9	1	4	3	8	2	7	6
7	4	2	6	5	1	9	8	3
8	6	3	2	9	7	5	4	1
1	3	7	8	2	6	4	5	9
6	5	4	7	1	9	3	2	8
9	2	8	3	4	5	6	1	7

Rocky Pictures (page 53)

8	1	7	5	2	3	9	6	4
3	4	6	9	1	8	7	2	5
2	5	9	7	4	6	3	1	8
1	7	3	2	6	4	8	5	9
4	8	2	3	5	9	1	7	6
9	6	5	8	7	1	4	3	2
6	2	8	4	3	7	5	9	1
5	3	4	1	9	2	6	8	7
7	9	1	6	8	5	2	4	3

Millions of Bison (page 54)

2	9	1	7	6	5	8	3	4
8	7	4	3	1	2	9	6	5
5	6	3	9	8	4	7	1	2
4	8	7	6	2	3	5	9	1
1	2	9	5	4	8	3	7	6
3	5	6	1	9	7	4	2	8
6	3	2	4	5	9	1	8	7
7	1	5	8	3	6	2	4	9
9	4	8	2	7	1	6	5	3

Standing Straight (page 55)

8	6	1	2	3	7	4	5	9
4	3	9	8	5	1	7	6	2
2	5	7	6	9	4	3	8	1
9	7	5	3	2	8	6	1	4
1	8	2	4	6	9	5	3	7
6	4	3	1	7	5	2	9	8
5	1	6	7	8	2	9	4	3
7	9	4	5	1	3	8	2	6
3	2	8	9	4	6	1	7	5

Northwestern Indians (page 56)

7	1	9	5	3	2	8	4	6
2	3	4	9	6	8	1	7	5
5	8	6	1	7	4	3	2	9
3	5	2	8	1	6	4	9	7
1	4	8	7	5	9	6	3	2
6	9	7	4	2	3	5	8	1
9	6	5	3	4	7	2	1	8
8	2	3	6	9	1	7	5	4
4	7	1	2	8	5	9	6	3

Animal Images (page 57)

3	9	2	5	7	6	4	8	1
4	1	8	9	2	3	6	5	7
6	7	5	8	4	1	9	2	3
9	5	3	7	8	2	1	6	4
8	4	6	3	1	9	2	7	5
7	2	1	4	6	5	8	3	9
2	3	7	1	9	8	5	4	6
1	6	4	2	5	7	3	9	8
5	8	9	6	3	4	7	1	2

Answer Key *(cont.)*

Powwow (page 58)

5	6	2	7	8	1	3	4	9
7	4	9	6	3	5	8	1	2
8	1	3	2	4	9	7	5	6
2	7	8	5	9	4	1	6	3
1	5	6	8	7	3	9	2	4
9	3	4	1	2	6	5	8	7
3	8	1	9	6	2	4	7	5
4	2	5	3	1	7	6	9	8
6	9	7	4	5	8	2	3	1

Roaming Spirit (page 59)

8	4	5	3	1	6	2	7	9
2	1	6	7	5	9	4	8	3
7	3	9	4	8	2	5	6	1
4	5	1	8	6	3	7	9	2
9	8	2	5	4	7	3	1	6
3	6	7	2	9	1	8	5	4
6	7	8	1	3	4	9	2	5
1	2	3	9	7	5	6	4	8
5	9	4	6	2	8	1	3	7

Painted Vessel (page 60)

2	7	3	4	8	6	9	5	1
6	5	9	7	2	1	4	3	8
1	8	4	3	5	9	2	7	6
8	9	7	6	3	5	1	2	4
3	1	2	8	9	4	5	6	7
5	4	6	2	1	7	3	8	9
9	2	8	1	7	3	6	4	5
4	3	1	5	6	8	7	9	2
7	6	5	9	4	2	8	1	3